Inside the Mind of

Shane Dawson

The Brain Institute for Studies on Intelligence

Made in the
USA
Middletown, DE

77376602R00116